Scavengers:
Eating Nature's Trash

Flesh Flies

Emma Carlson Berne

PowerKiDS press.

New York

Published in 2015 by The Rosen Publishing Group, Inc.
29 East 21st Street, New York, NY 10010

First Edition

Editor: Joanne Randolph
Book Design: Joe Carney
Photo Research: Katie Stryker

Photo Credits: Cover, p. 6 PHOTO FUN/Shutterstock.com; p. 5 Nigel Cattlin/Visuals Unlimited/Getty Images; p. 7 Mauvries/iStock/Thinkstock; p. 8 Douglas Philipon/iStock/Thinkstock; p. 9 Iurii Konoval/Shutterstock.com; p. 10 Valter Jacinto/Flickr Open/Getty Images; pp. 11, 22 bahadir-yeniceri/iStock/Thinkstock; p. 12 Jaroslaw Wojcik/iStock/Thinkstock; p. 13 Andy Nowack/iStock/Thinkstock; p. 14 Visuals Unlimited, Inc./MarkPlonsky/Getty Images; p. 15 Flickr/Getty Images; p. 16 Dr. James L. Castner/Visuals Unlimited/Getty Images; p. 17 Sarah Marchant/Shutterstock.com; p. 18 Robert Burns/iStock/Thinkstock; p. 19 Achim Prill/iStock/Thinkstock; p. 20 Nathalie Speliers Ufermann/Shutterstock.com; p. 21 Elliotte Rusty Harold/Shutterstock.com.

Library of Congress Cataloging-in-Publication Data

Berne, Emma Carlson, author.
 Flesh flies / by Emma Carlson Berne. — First edition.
     pages cm — (Scavengers, eating nature's trash)
 Includes index.
 ISBN 978-1-4777-6588-3 (library binding) — ISBN 978-1-4777-6590-6 (pbk.) — ISBN 978-1-4777-6589-0 (6-pack)
 1. Sarcophagidae—Juvenile literature. 2. Maggots—Juvenile literature. 3. Ecology—Juvenile literature. 4. Scavengers (Zoology)—Juvenile literature.
 [1. Flies.] I. Title.
 QL537.S25B47 2015
 595.7715—dc23
                              2013046800

Manufactured in the United States of America

CPSIA Compliance Information: Batch #WS14PK6: For Further Information contact Rosen Publishing, New York, New York at 1-800-237-9932

Contents

Nature's Janitors

Eating dead flesh sounds gross, right? There are many animals that do just that, though. They eat dead animals and rotting vegetable matter. These animals are called **scavengers**, and they are nature's janitors. Without them, there would be a lot more dead animal **carcasses** lying around. That really would be gross.

Flesh flies are one of these scavengers. They look for dead animals and plants that are rotting. Then, they eat juices from the plants and animals. Flesh flies also place their **larvae** on dead animals. These larvae are sometimes called maggots. The maggots eat the dead animal flesh and grow into adult flies.

Flesh flies are insects, which means they have six legs and three main body parts. These are the head, thorax, and abdomen. They have large compound eyes, antennae, and wings, too.

Where Are the Flesh Flies?

There are lots of different kinds of flesh flies in the world. In fact, there are more than 2,000 **species**! The United States has more than 300 species alone.

Flesh flies can live in many different **climates**. They live in all US states, including chilly Alaska. They like warm, damp places best, though. Dead animals rot more easily there, and the flies can feed on them.

Flesh flies are common throughout the world. This flesh fly is dining on a dead insect larva.

Flesh flies can be recognized by their striped bodies and red eyes. If you are looking at a fly that has a shiny exoskeleton, then you are looking at a different kind of fly!

Not all flesh flies live on rotting flesh. Some species place their larvae in open wounds on living animals. Some live in **feces**. Some others are **parasites** on other live insects.

A Seat Near the Food, Please

Flesh flies like to live near their food. They hang out near dead animals, landfills, overflowing trash cans, or anywhere that dead animals and rotting plants are likely to be found. Slaughterhouses, where animals are killed for meat, have a hard time keeping flesh flies away.

Compost piles and dumps or landfills are often home to flesh flies and likely other kinds of flies, too.

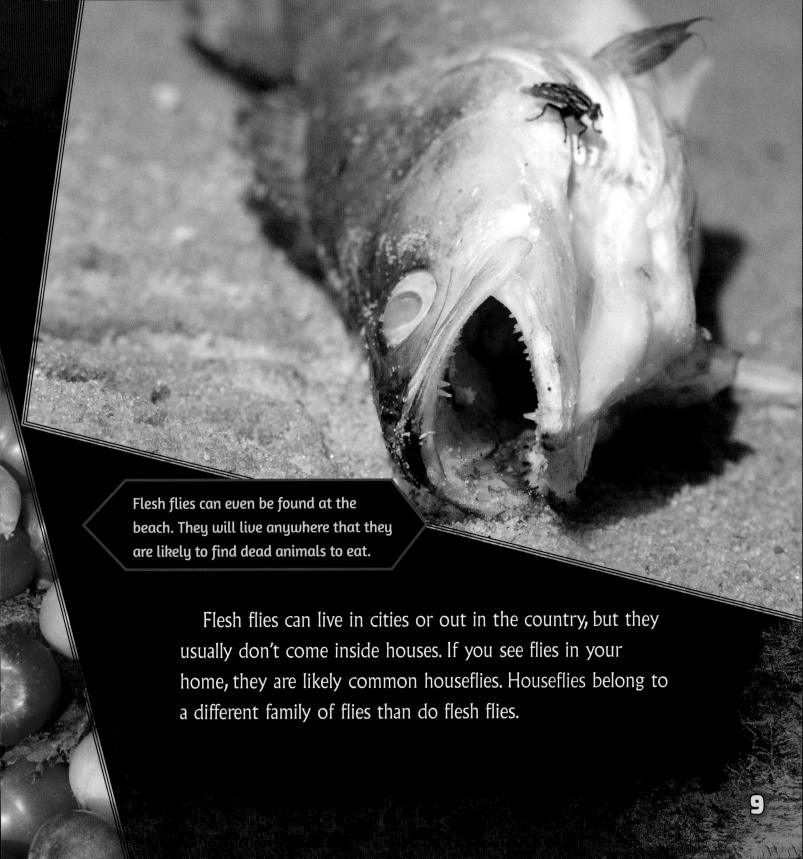

Flesh flies can even be found at the beach. They will live anywhere that they are likely to find dead animals to eat.

Flesh flies can live in cities or out in the country, but they usually don't come inside houses. If you see flies in your home, they are likely common houseflies. Houseflies belong to a different family of flies than do flesh flies.

How Do I Look?

Adult flesh flies are pretty ordinary looking. They are medium-sized flies at about .5 inch (1.3 cm) long. They have gray and black stripes running down their bodies and big, red eyes. Some have red bulges at the ends of their abdomens. Flesh flies have two pairs of wings, like all flies.

Flesh flies look a lot like other kinds of flies. Can you see this flesh fly's gray and black stripes and red eyes? Flesh flies, like other flies, have transparent wings, which means you can see through them.

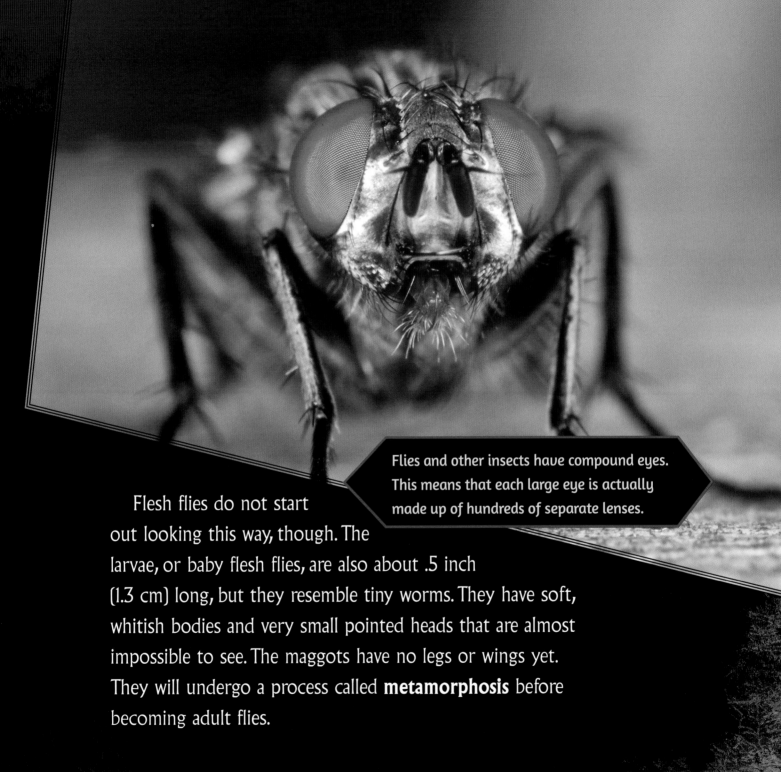

Flies and other insects have compound eyes. This means that each large eye is actually made up of hundreds of separate lenses.

Flesh flies do not start out looking this way, though. The larvae, or baby flesh flies, are also about .5 inch (1.3 cm) long, but they resemble tiny worms. They have soft, whitish bodies and very small pointed heads that are almost impossible to see. The maggots have no legs or wings yet. They will undergo a process called **metamorphosis** before becoming adult flies.

From Maggot to Fly

All flesh flies begin as an egg inside a female flesh fly. The eggs hatch inside the female. Then she deposits the living larvae onto a dead animal. The maggots feed on the dead flesh for about three to four days. Then they wiggle away to **pupate**. They can travel up to 100 yards (91 m), or about the length of a football field.

Unlike most flies, flesh flies do not lay their eggs on dead animals. They put their already-hatched larvae on the food. This means their babies can get right to work eating their disgusting meal!

It is hard to believe that these little worms (left) will ever look like this adult fly (above). Many insects undergo metamorphosis to achieve their adult form.

A larva forms a case around itself. Now the larva has become a **pupa**. The pupa stays inside the case for about 10 days, transforming into a fly. Then it emerges, fully adult and ready to produce larvae of its own.

Special Mouths for Special Food

Some flies bite and have mouthparts that allow for that. Flesh flies don't bite, though, so they don't have biting mouthparts. Instead, they have mouths that are like sponges. These sponging mouthparts are good for absorbing and sucking up the liquid juices of dead animals and dead plants. The saliva of the flies helps dissolve whatever food the fly wants to eat. Then the sponging mouthparts draw the liquid matter into the fly's body.

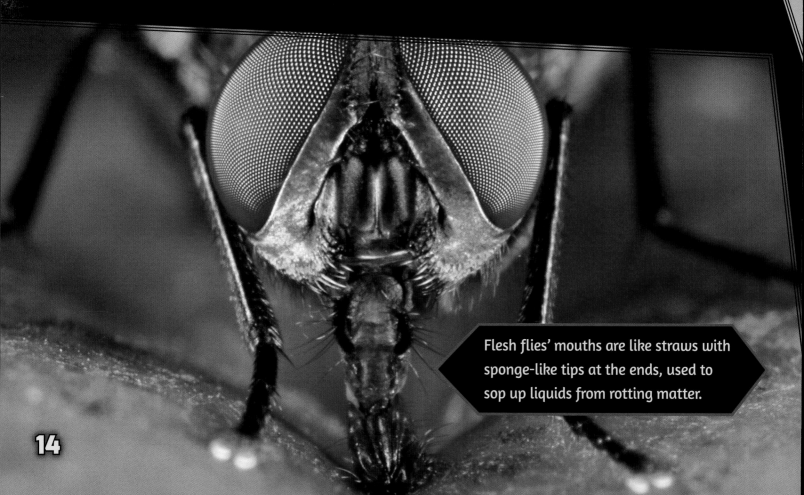

Flesh flies' mouths are like straws with sponge-like tips at the ends, used to sop up liquids from rotting matter.

Flesh flies blow bubbles after they eat to help digest or break down their food. They do this to let some of the liquid go back into the air so they get more concentrated nutrients from the food.

Maggots are a little different. They have hooks on their mouthparts. They use these hooks to break up the animal flesh so that they can eat it better.

Dead Animals Are Delicious

If you were a flesh fly, your favorite meal might be a nice squished squirrel. Flesh flies love to eat dead animal flesh from mammals, insects, reptiles, and birds.

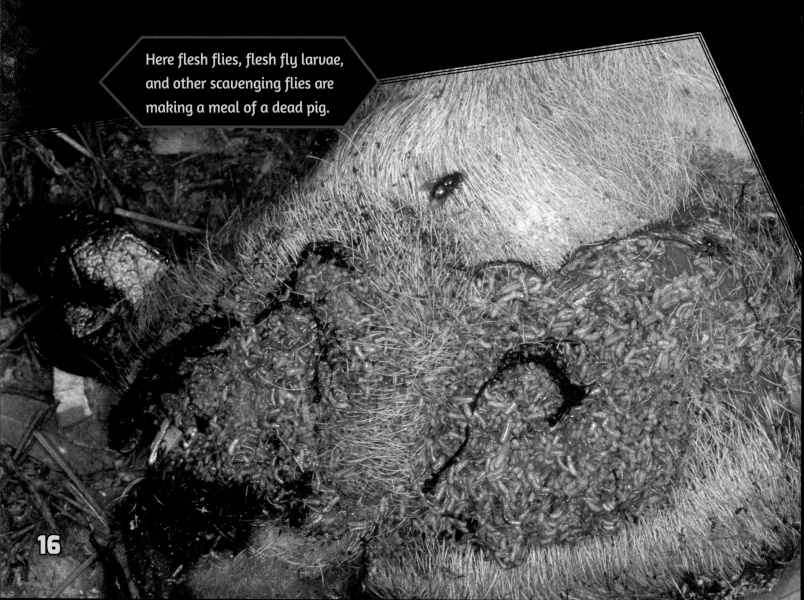

Here flesh flies, flesh fly larvae, and other scavenging flies are making a meal of a dead pig.

Flesh flies are not picky. They will feed and deposit larvae on most any kind of dead animal they can find.

Flesh flies like to feed only on animals that have been dead a short while, though. After a couple of weeks, the dead animal becomes too dry for the flesh flies to eat and they will leave. Crime investigators can even learn how long a body has been dead by examining the types and ages of maggots and flies that are feeding on it.

Rotting Fruit Is Tasty, Too

This flesh fly is eating a rotting fig.

Both flesh fly adults and larvae eat rotting meat. Adult flesh flies will eat other foods, too, though. They are happy to make a meal of rotting fruits or vegetables.

Pretty much any food, plant or animal, that is decomposing, or breaking down, is alright with flesh flies.

Adult flesh flies are not always eating disgusting, rotting food. Adult flesh flies will sip nectar from flowers, too.

Because adult flesh flies have mouths like sponges, they need to eat a liquid diet. They cannot bite pieces off of their food. Old fruit and vegetables provide lots of juices for them to suck up. Sometimes, adult flesh flies will drink nectar from flowers also.

Wait a Minute! This Is a Cactus!

Some **cacti** have flowers that smell just like rotting meat. Flesh flies buzz around the flowers, **pollinating** the cacti. They also deposit their larvae on the blooms, thinking they're on rotting meat. The maggots can't eat the flower and die quickly.

Klepto-What?

Flesh flies are scavengers, but they sometimes go by another name. They are sometimes called **kleptoparasites**. This means they steal or take something that belongs to another animal.

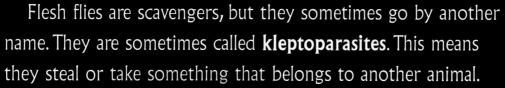

Some flesh flies lay eggs or deposit live young on dead or living insects.

Solitary bees and wasps, such as this thread-waisted wasp, are common victims of flesh flies that practice kleptoparasitism.

For some animals, this means that they might steal another animal's food. For flesh flies, it means that some of the species attack other living insects, such as bees and wasps. They place their larvae on the other insect. The larvae develop on the insect and then feed on its flesh. This differs from what regular parasites do, as normally parasites do not kill their hosts.

Maggot Therapy

Maggots can help people who have been wounded. Doctors sometimes place special **sterile** maggots in people's wounds. The maggots "clean" the wound by eating only the dead flesh and leaving the healthy flesh.

21

We Need Flesh Flies

Many people think that flies and maggots are gross. Flesh flies are actually very helpful to our planet, though. These important scavengers are nature's cleanup crew. They help get rid of the billions of animal and insect carcasses that would otherwise litter Earth.

Without scavengers like flesh flies, these bodies would take much longer to **decompose**. That would not make our planet a nice one to live on. Next time you see a flesh fly, don't swat it, thank it!

The flesh fly's family name is Sarcophagidae. This comes from the Greek words *sarco*, which means "flesh," and *phage*, which means "to eat."

Glossary

cacti (KAK-ty) Plants that have sharp needles instead of leaves and that are usually found in hot, dry places.

carcasses (KAR-kus-ez) Dead bodies.

climates (KLY-muts) The kinds of weather certain places have.

decompose (dee-kum-POHZ) To rot.

feces (FEE-seez) The solid waste of animals.

kleptoparasites (klep-toh-PER-eh-syts) Animals that take food that other animals have caught or collected or that place their larvae on other animals in order to feed on them.

larvae (LAHR-vee) Animals in the early period of life in which they have a wormlike form.

metamorphosis (meh-tuh-MOR-fuh-sus) A complete change in form.

parasites (PER-uh-syts) Living things that live in, on, or with other living things.

pollinating (PAH-luh-nayt-ing) Spreading pollen from one plant to another so that the plants can reproduce.

pupa (PYOO-puh) The second stage in the life of an insect that undergoes complete metamorphosis. Pupae generally do not feed or move.

pupate (PYOO-payt) To change from a larva to an adult.

scavengers (SKA-ven-jurz) Animals that eat dead things.

species (SPEE-sheez) One kind of living thing. All people are one species.

sterile (STER-ul) Free from germs.

Index

Websites

Due to the changing nature of Internet links, PowerKids Press has developed an online list of websites related to the subject of this book. This site is updated regularly. Please use this link to access the list: www.powerkidslinks.com/scav/flies/